COMMON SENSE

2024

THE CHILDREN'S VERSION

THOMAS PAINE JR

Common Sense 2024

Thomas Paine Jr.

An election was won
just four years ago...

by a candidates promise
to hand out some
dough.

To every person
went a stimulus check;

a few short months later,
the economy is a wreck.

This did not happen
while President Trump was
the boss.

America's hard working families
are now paying the cost.

Having to choose
on which bills to pay.

Why does the left side
think that this is okay?

Now comes the time
for an election once more...

God only knows
what we are in for.

With the blindfold removed
from our justice scale,

a three decade old story
or a persons tall tale?

When free speech costs millions
in court costs and fines,

President Trump is still fighting hard
for families like mine.

President Trump fights
for our rights,
for both you and for me.

He stands up to the foe
with the voice of the free.

President Trump will make
our southern border secure.

Guests are still welcome...
but they must use the front door.

The Media all say,
"45 is the worst!"

Yes even they
Deceiving America
are under Sleepy Joe's Curse.

A government of the people,
by the people , and for the
people,
is how it was intended to be.

Not a sly group of dictators
in a place called D.C.

The donkeys will kick
and the gators will chomp.

Pull up your
chair
to watch Trump drain the swamp.

President Trump will do this for you...
and
with an
USA

Please choose the Right one
on Election Day!

www.ingramcontent.com/pod-product-compliance
Lightning Source LLC
Chambersburg PA
CBHW082015160726
47999CB00008B/2821